Name	Wishes and Comments

Name	Wishes and Comments

Name	Wishes and Comments

Name	Wishes and Comments

Name	Wishes and Comments

Name	Wishes and Comments
Name	Wishes and Comments
Name	Wishes and Comments
Name	Wishes and Comments

Name	Wishes and Comments

Name	Wishes and Comments

Name	Wishes and Comments

Name	Wishes and Comments

Name	Wishes and Comments
Name	Wishes and Comments
Name	Wishes and Comments
Name	Wishes and Comments

Name	Wishes and Comments

Name	Wishes and Comments

Name	Wishes and Comments

Name	Wishes and Comments

Name	Wishes and Comments

Name	Wishes and Comments

Name	Wishes and Comments

Name	Wishes and Comments

Name	Wishes and Comments
Name	Wishes and Comments
Name	Wishes and Comments
Name	Wishes and Comments

Name	Wishes and Comments
Name	Wishes and Comments
Name	Wishes and Comments
Name	Wishes and Comments

Name	Wishes and Comments
Name	Wishes and Comments
Name	Wishes and Comments
Name	Wishes and Comments

Name	Wishes and Comments
Name	Wishes and Comments
Name	Wishes and Comments
Name	Wishes and Comments

| Name | Wishes and Comments |

| Name | Wishes and Comments |

| Name | Wishes and Comments |

| Name | Wishes and Comments |

Name	Wishes and Comments

Name	Wishes and Comments

Name	Wishes and Comments

Name	Wishes and Comments

Name	Wishes and Comments

Name	Wishes and Comments

Name	Wishes and Comments

Name	Wishes and Comments
Name	Wishes and Comments
Name	Wishes and Comments
Name	Wishes and Comments

Name	Wishes and Comments

Name	Wishes and Comments

Name	Wishes and Comments

Name	Wishes and Comments

Name	Wishes and Comments

Name	Wishes and Comments

Name	Wishes and Comments

Name	Wishes and Comments

Name	Wishes and Comments

Name	Wishes and Comments
Name	Wishes and Comments
Name	Wishes and Comments
Name	Wishes and Comments

Name	Wishes and Comments

Name	Wishes and Comments

Name	Wishes and Comments

Name	Wishes and Comments

Name	Wishes and Comments

Name	Wishes and Comments

Name	Wishes and Comments

Name	Wishes and Comments
Name	Wishes and Comments
Name	Wishes and Comments
Name	Wishes and Comments

Name	Wishes and Comments

Name	Wishes and Comments
Name	Wishes and Comments
Name	Wishes and Comments
Name	Wishes and Comments

Name	Wishes and Comments

Name	Wishes and Comments

Name	Wishes and Comments

Name	Wishes and Comments

Name	Wishes and Comments
Name	Wishes and Comments
Name	Wishes and Comments
Name	Wishes and Comments

Name	Wishes and Comments
Name	Wishes and Comments
Name	Wishes and Comments
Name	Wishes and Comments

Name	Wishes and Comments

Name	Wishes and Comments

Name	Wishes and Comments
Name	Wishes and Comments
Name	Wishes and Comments
Name	Wishes and Comments

Name	Wishes and Comments
Name	Wishes and Comments
Name	Wishes and Comments
Name	Wishes and Comments

Name	Wishes and Comments

Name	Wishes and Comments

| Name | Wishes and Comments |

| Name | Wishes and Comments |

| Name | Wishes and Comments |

| Name | Wishes and Comments |

Name	Wishes and Comments

Name	Wishes and Comments

Name	Wishes and Comments

Name	Wishes and Comments

Name	Wishes and Comments

Name	Wishes and Comments

Name	Wishes and Comments
Name	Wishes and Comments
Name	Wishes and Comments
Name	Wishes and Comments

Name	Wishes and Comments
Name	Wishes and Comments
Name	Wishes and Comments
Name	Wishes and Comments

Name	Wishes and Comments

Name	Wishes and Comments
Name	Wishes and Comments
Name	Wishes and Comments
Name	Wishes and Comments

Name	Wishes and Comments

Name	Wishes and Comments

Name	Wishes and Comments
Name	Wishes and Comments
Name	Wishes and Comments
Name	Wishes and Comments

Name	Wishes and Comments

Name	Wishes and Comments

Name	Wishes and Comments

Name	Wishes and Comments

Name	Wishes and Comments

Name	Wishes and Comments

Name	Wishes and Comments

Name	Wishes and Comments

Name	Wishes and Comments

Name	Wishes and Comments

Name	Wishes and Comments

Name	Wishes and Comments

www.ingramcontent.com/pod-product-compliance
Lightning Source LLC
LaVergne TN
LVHW072012060526
838200LV00011B/335